Peter Grayman

MY HAPPY BEES

2nd Edition

Simple and effective techniques of my practical beekeeping

How I made the Bees Happy

COPYRIGHT

DISCLAIMER
This book is provided for informational purposes only.
In this book, the author in art form outlined his original
practical approaches and non-standard views on some questions
of home beekeeping.
This book is not a textbook or scientific work.
You must understand that I set out my experience here, not a
piece of professional advice to use. You and only you are fully
responsible for the use and application of the information in this
book.
Under no circumstances will the author be liable to any party for
any direct, indirect, special or other indirect damage as a result
of any use of the information set forth in this book.

PHOTO DISCLAIMER
All pictures and photos are used exclusively for a visual
illustration of the content contained in the text.

DEDICATION

With gratitude, I dedicate this book to my dear and beloved father, teacher and mentor

MY THANKS

This book would not have been written without my beloved wife Guzel. Her unsurpassed goodness has given me strength and creative inspiration.

I sincerely thank to my son Anton, who with his attention to detail has helped me in the work to improve the text and content of this book.

I am grateful to my friend Andrey, for his enthusiasm and encouragement which helped my book project to move forward.

I am grateful to my friend Alexei for his sincere and unwavering support of my project. Thank you, friend, for moral support, which filled my heart with confidence and faith.

I sincerely thank to my friend Sverre, he was the first reader to write the first and, at the same time, an excellent review of my book. His enthusiasm and admiration gave me an indescribable feeling of happiness. Thank you so much, Sverre.

Special thanks deserves Prokopenko Olga, who has done a titanic work on editing and correcting my "super" English writing.

To all the people who have put part of their soul into this book, and to readers who will read it to the end: big and sincere gratitude!

CONTENTS

PREFACE

Dear reader, in front of you is the second edition of the book. It is not like any other beekeeping book. This is not a textbook or a practical guide in the usual interpretation.

I didn't try to challenge myself providing the reader with a comprehensive treatise on beekeeping. Plenty of such books already exist. I have outlined only the most important findings based on my learnings and experiences. The ones that, in my opinion, helped my bees and me find happiness in life.

The information contained in the book will be useful for both experienced and novice beekeepers. Everyone will discover for themselves interesting "goodies". For instance: the way I have changed the quality of bees life, the way I have protected them from exposure to electrical fields, and what methods of Varroa mite fight I applied to.

Some of the described findings and techniques are often overlooked even by proficient beekeepers, who often consider them to be of secondary importance whereas most beginners do not even consider them at all. You will see how simple, at first glance, actions (e.g. beehives coloration) can significantly change the mood and health of a colony of bees.

Among other things, you will learn my completely new method of dividing the family of bees into two equal parts without losing the bees flying for a nectar (flight bees). You will learn how I harvest honey, how I brew a tasty and useful feed for bees, how and where I place hives and a lot of other practical information, which is important not only for bees but also can become a business springboard for the enterprising reader...

Besides all this, I suggest an unusual idea, an unusual reason for conducting beekeeping. This idea is fundamentally changing the relationship between beekeeper and bee, filling their relationship with mutual love and respect. Gives the beekeeper an opportunity to feel involved in bee magic. Fills beekeeper heart with meaning and the joy of being alive. This feeling warms the heart and pleases the soul. And this wonderful sensation can settle in your heart as well. This is beautiful, isn't it?!

I believe that when this idea prevails among beekeepers, our world, our Earth as a whole will be happier and kinder.

I will be elated if my practical findings prove to be useful and will bring prosperity to you and your bees. The more cheerful bees are, the more harmony and love occur in our World. Make your bees glad and join with them in a Song of Love and a Song of Joy.

Welcome to my Happy Bees.

NECESSARY NOTES BY THE AUTHOR

"For a better life in the world!"
Words from a song

All that I wrote in this little book can be called a treasure chest of my experience. These "discoveries" did not collapse of the sky one day. All of them appeared in my piggy bank and gradually have been found in the difficult experiences, in my mistakes and failures, in communion with other beekeepers, textbooks and books on beekeeping.

I've been familiar with bees since my childhood, as my father had a small apiary. From the early age, I was involved in the work on the apiary but did not show a lot of interest.

What can you expect from a ten-year-old boy who does not think about bees, but about radio details and radio receivers? By the way, my first transistor radio receiver, I assembled being 11 years old, and the detector one even before that age.

My father loved bees and all his free time he devoted to his "pets". I was just his assistant. I think that I was a good helper, although my interests laid entirely in a different field.

Soon after my father passed away, the bees turned out to be orphans, and I was forced to do the work on the apiary. So unexpectedly even for myself, I set foot on the way of beekeeping. It is so crucial for further understanding of all that is written in this section.

This state of affairs has greatly complicated my life. By that time, I knew a lot out of practice, but I had very little theoretical knowledge.

It's one thing when you gradually develop in beekeeping and your apiary is growing along with your experience. It's quite another matter when you get a large number of hives at once.

I looked like a bad swimmer, who was thrown in the water far from the shore. I will not describe all my difficulties, failures and mistakes. I will say briefly. With great difficulty, I did not drown with my bees.

In the beginning, it was difficult not only because I did not know a lot, but also because I was compelled to do this. I think you understand me.

All of you know perfectly well that the work of a beekeeper is troublesome and consists not only from the process of extracting honey from hives. Although, many average consumers think so.

I had such situations when it was necessary to take urgent measures, but I did not know how to do it. And not to do on or postpone it was impossible. There was no knowledge in this field, there was no experience and there was no one to ask. There were no cell phones in those days. Such situations were extremely difficult. Probably every beekeeper had such difficult professional situations.

It was at such moments that a treacherous question appeared in my head, but why should I do all this stuff? Sometimes I was in despair and I wanted to give everything up and forget it. However, something kept me away from such a radical step.

Now when I have become completely gray, I understand that it was the good memory of my father that was giving me strength in those difficult days of my "swimming" without a lifebuoy

Years passed. The experience was acquired. Knowledge accumulated. Over time, I felt affection for my bees, but the question: "Why do I keep bees?" kept on my alert and did not give me rest. Honey, as an incentive, did not interest me. The concept of responsibility before my father's case, over time, lost its relevance because the bees had already become mine.

I needed the answer, to determine the appropriateness of my occupation. I wanted to find an important reason, based on which, I could continue beekeeping activities. After all, deep down I did not want to give up this noble cause.

I cannot remember how it happened that the answer dawned on me. Probably, it happened after I decided to keep the bees all right for the world to become a better place. Or maybe the decision was made on the basis of the answer that came along.

Having answered to my question, I put everything in its place. I sighed with relief, I had a goal, I found for myself the meaning of my beekeeping activities.

From now on, I will be engaged in beekeeping so that surrounding nature will blossom with harmony and happiness. To make the world a better place.

My bees will work tirelessly on this, and I am going to help them with all my strength and abilities, to the best of my knowledge and skills.

From this moment on my attitude to bees has changed, and I assure you, the attitude of my bees to me has become much warmer and kinder. You yourself will be convinced in it after reading the book till the end.

Everything I wrote about in it below was applied for my bees, and, it seems to me, they became the happiest ones on the whole planet Earth. Of course, not taking into consideration those who live free lives in natural conditions. Although, how to say?

I tried to make living conditions for my bees no worse than the ones of wild bees. At the same time, they have my care and love, at the same time wild bees are deprived of such care. So, who is happier, wild bees or mine, this is a contentious issue. It's up to you to decide (The solution to this problem is at the end of the book).

You may laugh, but I call my apiary the freest apiary in the World. I do not bother bees with frequent examinations and regular extraction of honey. My bees live in pleasure, they are happy and quietly perform the tasks of harmonizing the surrounding nature.

Personally I, at the same time, feel satisfaction from being aware of involvement in the bee magic, which fills the world with love and harmony of life.

All this I set out for the full understanding of what I'm writing in this book, for understanding my approach to bees and the world around me.

And I also wanted to draw your attention to the fact that the very idea of breeding bees for the sake of improving our environment is not meaningless and has the right to exist.

I offer readers an unusual idea, an unusual reason for starting a beekeeping business.

I propose to make the main motive for practicing beekeeping a desire to improve the world around us with the help of bee colonies.

This approach does not require a refusal to receive honey, no. However, it radically changes the relationship between the beekeeper and the bees. With this attitude, a bee becomes a center of attention, and honey - the result of its action.

This approach allowed me to make my bees happy. My bees calmly perform the tasks of harmonizing the surrounding nature. I am also pleased to realize my involvement in bee magic, which fills the world with love and harmony of life. This feeling warms my heart and pleases my soul. And this wonderful feeling can settle in your hearts as well. It's wonderful, isn't it?

I believe that when this idea prevails among beekeepers, our World, our Earth as a whole will be happier and kinder. What do you say to that? I personally like this idea.

Make your Bees Happy, and they will reveal to you
The Joy of Life!

HOW TO MAKE BEES HAPPY?

" If I knew how to do this,
I would have done it right now "

For successful beekeeping, a beekeeper needs to know and understand many questions related to bees and not only.

A beekeeper must know the diseases of bees and the methods of treatment, understand the biology and physiology of the bee species in particular and the bee family as a whole unity. To know the techniques and ways of treatment for bees living in hives, to be able to build and repair their hives, to know how and when to extract honey. And this is not a complete list of all what a beekeeper should know and be able to do.

I do not set myself the task of covering these and other issues of practical beekeeping. I just want to emphasize the fact that a beekeeper needs to have a great erudition. All these questions are to some extent expounded in a variety of books on beekeeping.

My dear readers, I want to draw your attention to very important issues of practical beekeeping. At first glance, these questions seem to be irrelevant.

These questions are often overlooked by many beekeepers, they consider them secondary and do not give them due attention. However, from further narration, you will learn that these moments are the fundamental ones in the matter of happiness and well-being of a bee family.

I suggest for a moment to get distracted. Let's fantasize a little and answer the question: "What does a person need to live a long and happy life?". Stop, please, for a moment and think it over. Count to ten.

I'm sure you already have got several answers. Very good. There below I answer to this question. You will be able to mentally compare your answers with mine and even discuss.

If we ask this question to a million people, we will get, no less, ten million answers. Analyzing them, we can identify a lot of common answers. All of them, to some extent, will be important and necessary to answer the question asked above.

Similarly, asking a million beekeepers the question: "How to make bees happy?", we will get, no less than a million different answers. And in this case, all of them will be important in answering our main question.

However, both among the answers to the first question, and among the answers to the second one, there are only a few fundamental answers or conditions. Without these basic things, in my opinion, a person cannot live a long and happy life, and bees cannot have all the fullness of their bee happiness.

I will take the floor and voice these crucial options for answering the questions asked above.

In the first case, in order to live a long and happy life, it is necessary and sufficient for a person to have:

1. A strong and healthy body;

2. An intelligent head, in which there are an objective, specific knowledge and skills;

3. Calm heart and a clear conscience.

All other answers will be in addition to these three. (I do not claim to be absolutely right.) This is only my point of view) Do not rush to refute my statement, especially since it does not directly relate to the subject and theme of bee happiness, but only indirectly.

As for the second question, then everything is much simpler and at the same time more complicated. Ideally, I emphasize, ideally, to make the bees happy they must be returned to the conditions of natural living. And left alone to the maximum.

However, we humans-beekeepers have moved bees to the hives not for the purpose to send them back to the forests and fields. And if the situation is so that we do not want to send our bees back to the forests and fields, then the conclusion suggests itself that we need to do so:

1. Create for bees the living conditions in our hives the same as in the hollows of living trees;

2. On a maximum leave them alone.

One of my acquaintances, an old beekeeper, used to say: "Do not disturb the bees, and they will not bother you." Perhaps, I did not accurately convey his statement, but I verified the truth of his words among my bees more than once.

So, I answered the question posed about happy bees and voiced the two main conditions necessary and sufficient for the successful and happy development of a bee family.

All other measures to care for bees are certainly no less important than these two, but all of them without exception are nothing but important additions to these two. This is my deep belief, based on my practice of beekeeping.

And so, the second position is easy to accomplish. For this, any beekeeper should reduce his zeal in constant and frequent inspections of bee colonies and increase his attention and observation.

How to fulfill the first advice? How to create conditions for the life of bees in our beehives that are the same as in hollows of living trees?

In order to do this, we need to identify the main difference featuring these homes. Why do bees in natural conditions arrange their nests, mainly in the hollows of living trees? Let's try to figure this out.

There are obviously many reasons for this. I'll now list the most important and, in my opinion, the main:

1. Bees can easily maintain a stable climate in such a dwelling at any time of the year.

2. A living tree provides bees with protection against excessive heat and cold.

3. The living tree "breathes", and this natural process of gas metabolism easily helps bees to get rid of excess carbon dioxide and moist air.

4. The bee family in the hollow is twice protected from the effects of electric fields. [1,2,3,4,5] The wood around the hollow protects the bees from the natural electric field of the Earth.

The tree crowns are charged with a negative charge and therefore protect the space of the forest and bees in the hollow from atmospheric electricity [2,3,4,5].

From this list it is clearly visible that we have deprived our bees, having moved them in beehives from dielectric materials such as dry wood or plastic.

We people and beekeepers fundamentally changed the natural habitat for bees. Our wooden beehives do not have the protective properties of a living tree. They are permeable to the electric field of the Earth, they cannot protect bees from atmosphere electricity and from the electromagnetic fields created by our modern civilization [6,7,8,9].

I hope that I managed to draw your attention to the fundamental moments necessary for bee happiness. And how, I managed to make my bees happy, you, my dear reader, will learn from the following narrative.

SUMMARY

For the successful and happy development of bee colonies, a beekeeper needs, first of all, to take care of the comfortable conditions for the bees in the beehive [15,16,17,18], and to leave them alone to the maximum,not interfering without a special need, in the life and work of a bee family.

HOW DID I CHANGE THE QUALITY OF BEES LIVING?

To radically improve the quality bees life, I had to apply a comprehensive approach to the modernization of my bee farm.

The first stage is a change in the physical properties of my hives. The second stage is the correct arrangement of the hives on the selected territory.

You will read about the disposition of the hives in the future, and now I will dwell in more detail on how I carried out the task of the first stage.

To complete the task of the first stage, it was needed, as far as possible, to bring the living conditions of the bees in my hives to living conditions in the hollow of a living tree.

To solve this problem, it was necessary:

1.To improve the temperature regime in the hive by protecting it from overheating;

2. Implement the protection of the surface of a hive from the external environment (rain, snow, humidity).

At the same time, to preserve the natural properties of wood.

It was important for me to preserve the ability of wood to produce gas exchange processes between the internal volume of the hive and the external environment, to preserve the ability of wood to get rid of moisture unhinderedly.

In other words, to enable the hive to "breathe" and at the same time not to lose the properties of the protective coating on the surface of the hive;

3. To provide bees with protection from the effects of electric fields.

It should be noted that all my hives by that time were painted with enamel paint in different colors.

What did I do?

First of all, gradually, the hive by the hive, I took off the enamel paint from the surface.

It was necessary to work hard, it is not an easy job. I used a simple brush, and an angular grinder, and all sorts of scrapers. The surface of the hives was cleaned to white wood.

Then I painted all my beehives with "special" paint.

Believe it or not, with such a simple action, I solved all the tasks of the first stage, and the special paint helped me in this, and this is not a simple paint, this special paint I made myself.

At first glance, the solution seems ridiculous, but let's not rush to conclusions. Let's understand everything in order and slowly.

What color of paint have I used?

You certainly know that bees can distinguish between Blue, Yellow, Black and White colors. Therefore, I limited myself to coloring my hives with this palette. Of course, black color for these purposes is completely useless, and I did not apply it.

I painted all of my beehives with white special paint of my own production. The area of the landing board I painted in blue or yellow color to facilitate the orientation of the bees. All these features of the appearance of my hives, you can see in the photo.

The white surface, as is known, perfectly reflects the sun's rays. In this simple way, I provided my bees with additional temperature comfort and implemented a solution to the problem of protecting bees from overheating on bright sunny days. Thus, the first item (see above) was completed, but not only the first item.

What paint did I use?

As I said above, to implement the protection of the surface of the hive from the external environment (rain, snow, humidity) and at the same time, to preserve the ability of wood to produce gas exchange processes between the internal volume of the hive and the external environment, at the same time preserve the ability of wood to get rid of moisture unhinderedly, I used all the properties of water-based acrylic dyes. In other words, these paints allow you to get a protective coating that allows the hive to "breathe".

I propose to consider in detail the properties of Acrylic paints useful for our bees. For the coloring of my hives, I used a paint based on an aqueous dispersion of acrylic latex. Acrylic paints for wood consist of an acrylic binder, pigment, water, and additives.

Acrylic paints practically do not have a smell, they are easy to use, easy to rinse off the instrument with water, quickly dry out. Acrylic paints perfectly tolerate external weather effects: temperature changes, high humidity, and direct sunlight. The paint protects the wood surface of the hive against rot and cracking.

In addition, these paints form a vapor-permeable film. The vapor permeability of the acrylic coating is a very important property for the surface of the hive. With this coating, the tree "breathes", and therefore there is a natural process of gas exchange of the internal volume of the hive with the external environment.

This useful property of acrylic dyes approximates the "climatic" conditions inside the hive to the conditions of life of bees in natural habitations. This is the first point.

The presence of a vapor-permeable surface in the acrylic coating makes it possible for wood to easily get rid of moisture, without the effect of peeling of the paint coating, as in the case of enamel or oil paints. This is the second point.

With acrylic paints it is easy to work, the process of staining is quick and pleasant. Anyone who has worked with these paints will confirm my words. Who had not worked, after testing this paint will agree with me. This is the third.

White acrylic paint is easy to impart the desired color with the appropriate dyes. This is the fourth.

White acrylic paint serves as an excellent reflector of sunlight. This is the fifth.

How and what for I perfected the paint?

And so, using all the above listed properties of acrylic water-based paint, I was able to improve the temperature regime in the hive, protect the surface of the hive from the external environment and at the same time maintain the natural ability of wood to carry out gas exchange processes, which is essential for healthy and natural climate inside a hive.

It remains to solve the third, no less important, the task of protecting bees from electric fields of various origins. Above, I wrote that inside a hollow, bees are protected twice. The volume of living wood around the hollow protects the bees from the natural electric field of the Earth [1,2,3,4,5] and the crowns of the trees themselves, charged with negative charges, protect the space of the forest and the bees in the hollow from atmospheric electricity [2,3,4,5].

A little remark.

In order not to turn my book into scientific work, I will not in this small narrative go into detailed scientific discussions of this and other physical phenomena. I did not set myself such a goal.

I brought in the book Internet links concerning all the questions that I am writing out. Using these Internet links, you can go to the Internet to deepen knowledge on the issues raised.

(Additional online link to a great selection of material: Electromagnetic fields impact the birds, bees, wildlife, and our environment. A small example of critical research that has been done on this issue. (https://ehtrust.org/science/bees-butterflies-wildlife-research-electromagnetic-fields-environment/))

Let us leave remarks and return to the birth of a special paint idea.

From literary sources, from popular science articles published in beekeeping journals and online resources on the topic of beekeeping, I knew a few, at first glance, scattered facts, one way or another, related to electric fields and bees.

The first fact: in this article " Beehives, Bees, and the Electric Field " Yu. K. Barbarovich mentions that in the French journal Science and Life (1985, No. 813), an article was published on aluminum multicase beehives, mass-produced by the company Sorel.

The second fact: One of my friends, an old sailor and an avid fan of the navigation development history and the navy, drew my attention to a very curious fact. He said that in the old days, at the beginning of the marine navigation, there was development in using a magnetic compass and to reduce the phenomenon of deviation, the compass case was made of bronze. In addition, the hull and the compass box itself were painted with paint, which was made on the basis of bronze powder. (Deviation - the error of the compass readings associated with the influence of external electric and magnetic fields on the compass needle).

The third fact tells that in one of the online publications, to protect the bees from electric fields, it was proposed to cover the surface of the hive with aluminum sheets.

The fourth Fact tells that on the Internet, I repeatedly met information that in beehives, which are painted with paint made on the basis of aluminum or bronze powder, bees collect more honey and have a peace-loving character, they are calm and even kind.

You see in all these cases aluminum or bronze is present. Bronze and aluminum have the same physical properties. Having combined all these facts in one tangle, I began my experiments.

And so, coating the surface with aluminum is not practical and expensive. And I decided to paint my beehives with a paint based on aluminum powder, but at the same time to make the paint not on the basis of varnish or oil, enamel paint, but on the basis of acrylic water-based paint.

I added a new quality to the properties of acrylic water-based paint that is beneficial to bees that is the ability to reduce the effect of electric fields on a family of bees.

Of course, painting the hive is less effective than coating the surface with aluminum sheets. Painting with aluminum paint does not allow to create a continuous protective layer of metal particles distributed in the dye volume.

However, I chose a surface painting because of the simplicity of the practical application and the universality of the results obtained.

After all, by this simple way, I managed to accomplish the task of the first stage, I managed to bring the living conditions of the bees in my hives to the living conditions in the hollow of a living tree.

What I've done? I added the aluminum powder to white acrylic paint. This gave the paint new properties. It is this paint, as I called earlier, not a simple paint, a special paint.

Water-based paint is usually quite thick. In order to make it more liquid, I added water.

You need to get such consistency to so that paint covers the surface in an even layer so that it lays on the surface easily and pleasantly and doesn't stiffen through the brush in thick stripes. So, it would be easy and pleasant to apply it to the surface of the hive. I think you understand me; the intuition will tell you.

I mixed the aluminum powder with the paint using an electric drill and a homemade simple whisk. You can take one whisk from a kitchen mixer.

How much did I add the aluminum powder in it? Again, intuitively, so that the white paint became light gray after the intense mixing.

A lot of powder cannot be here. Of course, moderation is important in everything. The gray color of my aluminum paint was so gray that I could, after drying, completely paint over it a pure white color.

The first layer was painted with special aluminum paint. Then, after the first layer of paint had completely dried, I applied a second layer of pure white paint. The second layer, without any metal powder, so that the surface became bright white.

The color of the white paint for coloring the front of the hive was changed using dyes designed specifically for this purpose. They are usually sold in the same place as water-based paint. If you ask, the seller will surely tell you the right choice.

SUMMARY

I painted all my hives with white water-based paint, with aluminum powder added in. The area of a bee-entrance was spotted with colors pleasant for a bee-eye such as yellow and blue. With these simple actions, I achieved four goals thereby, bringing the living conditions of bees in a hive closer to the natural living conditions in a hollow:

1. I managed to protect bees from electric fields [1,2,3,4,5,6,7,8,9];

2. I managed to improve the temperature regime in the hive, as the white coating of the entire surface prevents overheating of the hive even on the hottest days;

3. I managed to provide bees with colored markers for additional orientation;

4. I managed to protect the surface of the hive from the external environment and at the same time maintain the natural ability of wood to carry out gas

exchange processes, which is essential for healthy and natural climate inside a hive.

5. I managed to provide a beautiful environmentally friendly coating of the beehive.

My hives after upgrading.

Such houses are very popular with my bees. Bees are very kind (absolutely not evil) and in gratitude, they collect generous harvests of honey for me.

Comparing the results of their work before and after staining my hives with an unusual "metallic" paint, I can say that the honey collection has more than doubled. And this is not boasting, but a life proved the fact.

As for my bees' even temper and their kind attitude towards me, believe it or not, many years in a row during the honey collection, I was not stung by my bees. There are, of course, cases, but this happens extremely rarely and mainly if I accidentally strangle a bee by hand. Even a little insulting that it happens this way. And then I'm outraged in jest, kind of where is APITHERAPY?

For the sake of justice, it should be noted that such a good-natured attitude of bees is caused not only by the painting of hives but also by other actions aimed at creating comfort conditions for my bees. About all the rest of my actions you will read further, in this little book.

Listening to their buzz, I try to treat them by bee-like. One may ask how is that? Yes, this means carefully and with love. I love them, and they pay it back.

As a confirmation of the words about the calm nature of my lucky bees here is a photo.

It's me, after only half an hour after honey extraction, I'm having a rest near my hives ...

Bees are absolutely quiet and disturb neither me nor my neighbors.

By the way about the neighbors. For all of their happy life, my bees have never bothered my neighbors. In any case, neighbors did not complain. This fact is another confirmation of the fact that happy bees do not care about neighbors. Happy bees have more important things to do - the job of improving the World.

With such a simple action as painting the surface of the hive with a not simple, but special paint, I brought the ecology of bees dwelling closer to the wildlife.

Unfortunately, for many beekeepers, a problem of the beehive coloration is not the number one priority in the list of important cases. Such beekeepers lose in the amount of collected honey, and bees cannot reach the state of their bee happiness and the Joy of Beeing.

HOW AND WHERE DID I LOCATE THE BEEHIVES?

From our hives location, it depends how the bees work and what they give to the beekeepers. The location of bee huts on the terrain affects the temperature regime, efficiency, mood and productivity of a bee family as a whole.

Therefore, how and where to place hives is the same important question for ensuring bee happiness, as well as the issue of staining.

In my opinion, it is important to optimally set the hive in the direction of north-south, while, if possible, provide bees with protection from external natural factors (sun, atmosphere electricity, geopathic zones. [10,11,12,13,14].

And so, let's take a closer look at how I set my hives, considering the above-stated tasks for providing bees with maximum comfort.

Installation of hives using a compass

How to establish the hives with respect to the north-south direction? On this account, each beekeeper has his own opinion. And those who begin their practice, often are confused by the variety of answers to this question.

I chose the answer for myself, based on common sense and logically justified arguments in favor of such a decision. I set all my hives to the north. And as it is demonstrated by the practice of using this method, the decision was right.

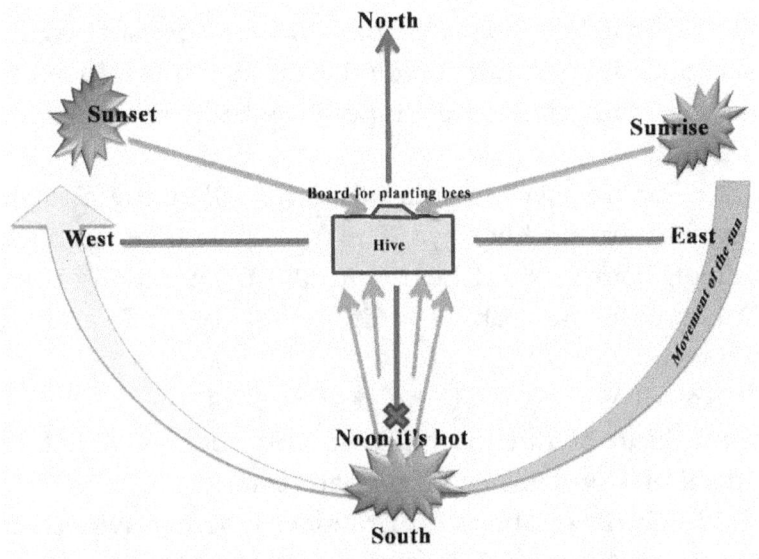

The scheme of my hives installation.

Here are the arguments in favor of this arrangement of the hives:

1. This position of a hive allows bees to use daytime most fully. The first rays of the rising sun motivate the bees to work. The rays of the evening sun stimulate the bees to continue working almost until sunset. Thus, the working time of a bee is almost doubled.

We can say with certainty that the bees, with such a disposition of a hive, works in two shifts.

The first shift, from sunrise to the moment when the nectar evaporates with the hot rays of the sun.

The second shift, from the moment when the sun's rays fall on the takeoff board on the west side, and until late at night.

And far beyond afternoon, when the sun again becomes affectionate, some flowers again produce the nectar and the bees happily gather the evening harvest.

2. Such a hives location does not allow them to get very hot during hot days. The front part hive, with the takeoff board, is not heated at all in the midday heat. This creates favorable conditions for the work and life of bees.

And if you protect the rear wall of the hive with some kind of mirror material, your bees will not be afraid of any heat, even in open terrain.

Watching my bees, in practice, I was convinced of the correctness of the above arguments.

The bees return, "loaded" with honey in the morning and evening. In this case, the intensity of the evening summer is much higher in those hives that are set "face" to the north.

Using this method of installing bee houses allows bees to collect much more honey. I am sure that my bees are grateful to me for this arrangement of their dwellings, and I am grateful to them for their generous harvests.

Beehives under the branches of trees

In the beginning, I already wrote that the tree crowns are charged with a negative electric charge and protect the forest space from atmospheric electricity [2,3,4,5].

Therefore, I installed my hives under the cover of trees and garden bushes.

And by this simple technique, I managed to protect the bees from the of atmospheric electricity and simultaneously from the hot rays of the midday sun.

So, what is very important, this way I managed to bring the living conditions of the bees in my hives to living conditions in the hollow of a living tree.

On the photo, you can see a small part of my bee yard. Hives are hidden under the branches of trees. And at this table, we often have picnics with friends or my family. Believe it or not, but the bees do not pay any attention at us. And when I've read in one reportage about how a journalist with a beekeeper was quietly having lunch at 20 meters from the hives, I could not help but smile. And this event was described as something unusual. Only twenty meters!

Too me it's a real achievement. My table is placed two meters from my hives, and I'm not bragging about it. And I write this only to once again draw your attention to the fact that happy bees do not care for people who do not disturb them.

Biolocation and my bees

From many beekeepers, I heard stories that supposedly, from the placement of a beehive the strength and productivity of a bee family depends a lot... They argued that there are places where bee colonies grow rapidly, gain strength, rarely swarm and bring a lot of honey. I think that many of you have paid attention to this.

At the beginning of my practice, there was such a case. One hive stood so that it kept bothering me while moving around with an inventory box and tools.

I just took it and moved it only one and a half meters to the side. You can say, instantly, within a week the situation in it has changed.

The bee queen almost stopped laying eggs, the activity of the bees decreased, while the bees in the other hives continued to work actively. I noticed that it was bad.

After two weeks of doubt, I replaced the hive to its original location. And what do you think? There was a miracle. It was hard to believe, but the fact was, as they say to the person.

The bees revived, the activity of the queen bee recovered. Then I explained the incident with the stories of old beekeepers (about bees' reproduction),

I had already heard. Due to my inexperience, and maybe for the other reasons, I did not pay attention to this occasion and simply forgot about it for many years.

Now I will digress a little from the topic of the narrative and briefly describe how I got acquainted with the method of Bilocation or Dowsing. [22]. This story will give me an opportunity to explain how I came back to that forgotten case with the rearrangement of the hive and how I applied the contemplation methods to my bees.

With this interesting phenomenon, I've got acquainted in the distant student years, when there was no mobile communication, the Internet and many common today's achievements of our civilization.

Funny student days.

Students are known to be curious and dedicated people. So, here I am, somehow (now I do not remember anymore) I was in the group of enthusiasts of historians-archaeologists. We were led, at that time, by a famous archaeologist. Unfortunately, his name has already been obliterated, but the fascination of his stories and active enthusiasm cannot be forgotten. He gathered around young guys and was spreading the idea of finding a legendary library of Yaroslav Mudryy. But my story is not about our adventures, but about an interesting and amazing way of finding objects and phenomenon that is invisible to a naked eye. Its name is bilocation or dowsing.

Preparing for such an exciting expedition, our group regularly made sorties into abandoned but preserved temple underground structures. Such places, in the vicinity of the K. city in those years, was of a great number.

I'm under the stone arch.

In one of the underground rooms.

That's where I met with the beautiful and mysterious word of Bilocation.

I looked with my own eyes, as the instructor showed " miracles " in searching of underground cavities. And then each of us had to try to do the same on our own. I do not know about others, but I would be extremely intrigued, and I have more than once convinced myself that the method works.

Wire rods confidently converged above the underground passages. It was so interesting that there were further experiments in the student hostel and outside it to search for electric wires, hidden objects, etc. and etc. It was interesting, fascinating and incomprehensible. How does it work?

Time flew by, the hobbies changed, the student's years were over, and the concept of "Bilocation" remained in memory, as an entertaining activity.

Being by nature a curious person, I periodically returned to this topic. I had to apply my little experience in this area to find the location of the water layers.

For the first time, with practical use, I used this method to find places for a water well in my yard.

That's when I remembered my student entertainment. It is made out from the wire two " L " - shaped twigs. They are also called the "Frame". I don't know why. For solidity, I guess.

Armed with these "instruments", I scanned the yard and indicated the location for the future well, as well as the depth to the water.

All my predictions have come true. The place was chosen, right. At this depth, my father and I reached the aquifer.

So once again I was convinced that the method works, despite the skeptical attitude of many theorists. I'm not a theoretical person, but a practitioner. Therefore, I just do things.

Then there was the experience of finding a place for a well for a friend. The place I selected coincided with the place, selected by the professionals, while water appeared to be in the depth detected by my frame. What is it? One may say a coincidence. Perhaps so, but I'm sure that the method does work.

I will not go into the theory of explaining (or in explaining the theory) of this method, especially since there are plenty of assumptions about this on the Internet. I repeat, I'm not a theorist, but a practitioner. That's actually the story of my acquaintance with this phenomenon and examples of its practical application.

Now let's go back to the bees and see how I applied these modest skills in this area to my bees. And whoever wants, he can apply this method to his bees.

I used to randomly dispose of my beehives on the piece of the area dedicated to this case. In the order, which, in my opinion, was determined by convenience in my work. But after my apiary began to be called the freest apiary in the World (how it happened, it is written in the section "Necessary explanation of the author"), I remembered the case with the hive rearrangement in an unfavorable place.

After pondering over this case, I decided to install the hives considering the so-called geopathic places, [10,11,12,13,14] using my skills in dowsing. For my bees live happily and nothing would bother them. In order to do this, I had to find my biographic "tools" and practice a little on the ground.

The task was to find not just a good place, but a good place for a particular hive.

I picked up my wire rods and thinking about a particular family of bees that is in a specific hive and set myself a searching task.

Mentally, the question was: "Where is the best place for bees right from this beehive?". Previously in my mind, the condition that the answer "YES" corresponds to the crossing of wire rods was set.

Moving along the territory, the place over which the twigs crossed was spotted. Then I repeatedly tested myself. As a result, the experiment showed that, indeed, for each individual bee family, a satisfactory place was found only one and it did not coincide with the rest of the bee colony. It turned out that, not even one of my hives was at its best place. I had to be rearranged to their optimal places.

I am quite sure that this method, connected with the exclusion of geopathic places for the arrangement of hives, has made a significant contribution to the well-being of my happy bees.

Practical advice for those who want to experiment

1. We make two such details. The size of a short bend is of the length of the palm and the long one is 3 -4times longer than a short bend.

2. Put the metal wire rods in hands, as in the photo.

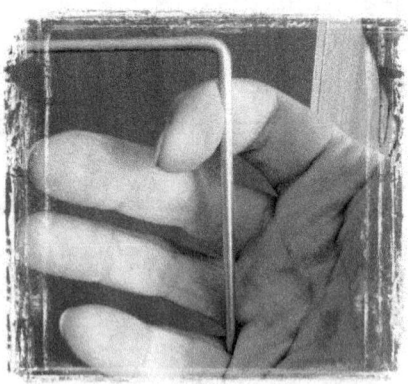

3. Without straining, we freely hold these metal wire rods, so that they easily rotate around the vertical axis.

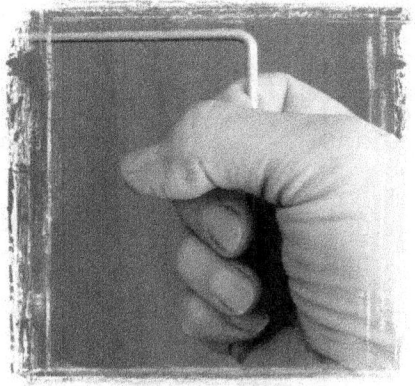

4. We bend our arms in the elbows. We freely press to the sides, and the hands with the metal rods directed forward. So that the long part of our rod is parallel to the surface of the earth. The distance between the wrists is 25-30 centimeters.

5. Mentally ask a search question. In my case, the question was: "Where is the best place for bees from this hive?". Preliminary, mentally put the condition that the answer "YES" corresponds to the crossing of metal wire rods.

We set mentally the searching task, we concentrate on this task and forward to the world of miracles and adventures.

For fun, you can try, experiment. It's just interesting. Undoubtedly, everything will work out. I did it and you will do it. Your bees will thank you.

SUMMARY

The efficiency and productivity of the bee family directly depends on where and how the hives stand. The location of bee huts on the terrain affects the temperature regime, efficiency, mood and productivity of a bee family as a whole.

I installation the Beehives:

1. "Face" strictly to the north;

2. Under the canopy of trees;

3. To find favorable locations using the biolocation method.

I am sure that this arrangement of hives is another reason why my bees are peaceful, collect a lot of honey and are not going to fly away, i.e. do not go into a swarm state.

The swarming of the bees is a separate topic and I am going to describe my views on this matter in the following narrative.

EXTRACTION OF HONEY

My little assistant. Perhaps the future beekeeper.

Necessary foreword

In the distant young years, when my father used to take me to the apiary as an assistant, I repeatedly had to observe the barbaric attitude of beekeepers to their bees.

I think that even now, such an attitude takes place, especially in large apiaries, where a bee is for a beekeeper, a "milk cow", a "machine" for the honey

4 3

production. Although the owners are much more humane to their cows than many "beekeepers" to their bees.

Anyone who has ever had the fortune to touch bees' honeycombs, to attend or personally examine a bee family, undoubtedly noticed a certain and, moreover, repeated order in the arrangement of frames with bee honeycombs. And this order reflects their contents. In a word, the beehive order reigns in the hive, and all the bees know what is what at home.

Now imagine the picture. There is a process of extracting honey from the apiary of 25 hives (several, but not a few - whoever harvested honey from at least 5 hives will understand what 20-25 hives mean). This is hard work for two beekeepers.

And that's what I had to observe repeatedly. From the hive, ALL (imagine, EVERYTHING) the honeycombs are removed and referred to the house for honey extraction. There they are prepared without any account and order for collecting.

All honey is taken, even from bee honeycombs, which contain bee brood, larvae, and eggs. Imagine when it killed more than one thousand bee eggs and larvae.

Then these desolate frames with bee honeycombs are referred to a bee house and completely randomly and quickly installed into the interior.

Can you imagine what is happening in a bee family after such an assault? The entire bee colonel is destroyed, there is no honey at all, half of the brood is absent, everything is turned upside down, a catastrophe ...

And so, misfortunate careless beekeepers carry out for their bees several times per season. After noisy may gardens there goes honey harvesting. After the blossoming acacia, linden, and buckwheat (whoever has it at hand) - each time honey is extracted, and each time catastrophes are repeated in bee colonies.

This attitude is simply a mockery. What kind of bee colony can survive it?

Then such beekeepers are surprised about the fact why their bees are so angry? Why do they sting neighbors? And do not let walk near their hives. Why do they swarm? Why are they so frail and worn out? Why are they flying away? And the answer is simple: "A dog is biting only because of a dog's life."

In my own way, being a child, I was worried about these unfortunate bees. Although my childhood experiences were short-lived, they nevertheless left their mark in my heart. And, obviously, they played an important role in the formation of my beekeeping views and beliefs.

Years passed, and by the will of fate, I became a beekeeper. Now I'm happy that I have favorite bees that harmonize the world around me, and I try to help them. The awareness of participation in this bee mission gives me strength and allows me to hope that I live my days in this world, not in vain.

Well, this is all the story, but the tale itself is ahead.

Now I will tell you how I harvest honey on my apiary. Where to begin? Probably, from the moment when it's time to collect honey.

In general, I took it as a rule to extract honey once per season, before preparing the families for wintering. As a rule, I do this after 10-15 August. I do not bother my bees with the process of obtaining honey. Therefore, my apiary is considered the freest apiary in the world.

However, there are exceptions. So, if the honey flow is good, and the bees simply have nowhere to store it, I have to pick up the excess and make room for the yield. And so, if there is a place for honey, I do not extract it and vice versa.

I will explain by example. May gardens faded. The weather was fine, the bees worked hard, and as a result, there is no empty space in the hives. What to do? I make an exception to these rules and take the excess as it frees up space for acacia, linden, and all of that is left in my garden.

I remember, once it was a good year, I had to extract honey after flowering acacia and after the linden, and then to prepare for winter. Such a case was only once in my practice. A rare phenomenon in our time.

However, I draw your attention, I do not take all the honey but only release the bee stores. What do you mean, I release bee-stores? Now we'll figure it out.

A few words about my methods of selecting frames with honeycombs for extracting honey. If I free space, then I take honey from the bee stores to the maximum. I draw your attention, I select honey only from pantries and leave nest stocks untouched.

I remembered my father's instructions well enough about the careful attitude to bee honeycombs with bee brood. In my practice, I have never taken or selected these honeycombs for honey extraction.

If I extract honey before preparing for wintering, then, of course, I do not become greedy and leave well-filled honey frames for my bees only. To me, there are surpluses which by all means are formed in the course of a winter bee nest formation. Often these pantries form a decent amount of honey. For which I always tell my bees THANKS.

My method of extracting honey

And so, the date of honey extraction is determined the day before, I do a survey of families in order to identify those frames with bee honeycombs, which the next day will go into processing.

Before beginning the inspection of the hive, I assign the number to each frame with bee's honeycombs.

For this purpose, I use paper scotch tape. It is convenient to make inscriptions on it, it sticks well and is easily removed. Numbering is necessary for me to restore the bee order after the end of the honey extraction process. Later, when I return honeycombs in a beehive, I will use numbers for installed them as before.

Then I do an inspection and select all honeycombs filled with honey and honeycombs with honey and pollen.

I just rearrange them in one direction, for example, in the "tail" and separate this warehouse from the nest by a partition or dividing board (diaphragm board). I hope that you understand me.

So, what do I get as a result? On the one hand, honeycombs with honey and brood are located, on the other side of the frame there are only ones with honey and frames with honey and pollen. During the night, the bulk of the bees moves to the nesting part, and on the selected bee honeycombs, the bees are almost absent. That's it, preparation is made.

The next morning, I begin the process of honey extraction, in fact, this is just the transfer of frames with honey cells to the extracting site.

The bees are absolutely calm because the nesting honeycombs are intact and the order is not broken there.

A small number of bees, which are present on honeycombs, are easily and painlessly shaken into the hive. Frames with bee honeycombs are sent into transport boxes. Further, the preparation of frames with bee honeycombs that is pruning of sealed cells. Then the honey extractor is used and back to the hive.

And here are the first "drops" of amazing honey.

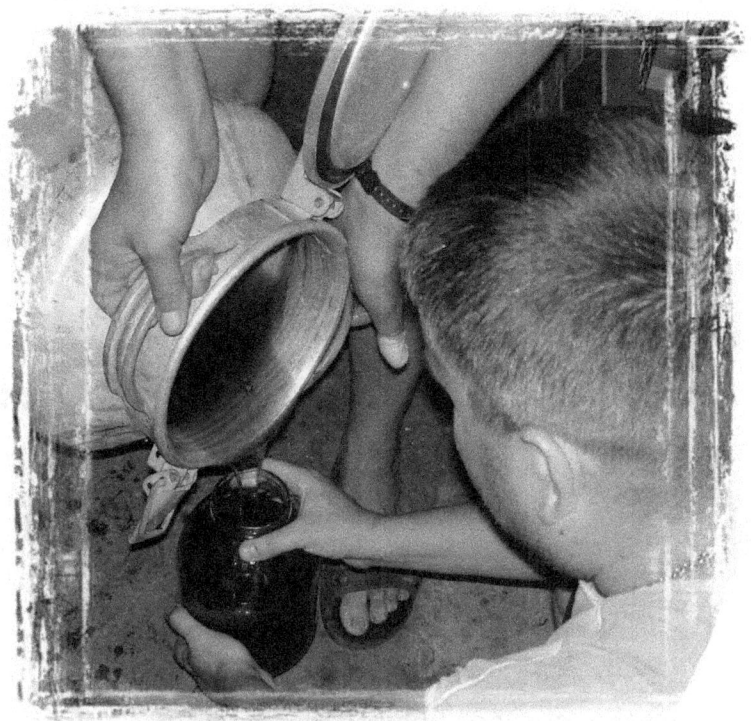

The work is almost finished. The last pot is filled
with amazing honey.

To speed up the general process of honey
extraction, when returning frames with bee
honeycombs back home, I do not regularize them by
numbers, but simply add them to the hive. They still
remain behind the dividing board. I do not remove the
dividing board. During the night, bees will clean the
honeycomb from the remnants of honey.

The next day, without hurrying without fuss, I will
install the frames with honeycombs in order of
numbers. I restore the bee's order and remove the
dividing board. Bees will be calm, peace-loving and

even grateful for the release of space for new honey. Thus, I extract honey away from my happy bees. And it seems to me that my bees even like this process.

Despite the fact that I have collected honey, the bees are completely peaceful and completely not evil.

I have already written, that my happy bees never sting me in the process of honey extraction. Believe it or not, I have to donate a pair of dozen bees from different hives for the organization of the therapeutic treatment process.

I catch bees with tweezers and lean them against my hands to receive their stings. Probably, it looks cruel on my part, but I must keep myself in shape.

SUMMARY

A few highlights of my method of honey collection:

1. Under no circumstances I take honey from the nesting part;

2. Wax honeycombs with brood and honey called a nest, on the eve of extracting I separate from the others by a partition;

3. The day after the extraction of honey, I set all the frames with honeycombs in their places and delete the dividing board.

With this method, the bees calmly tolerate the process of extracting honey. Bees behaving near the hives calmly and peacefully. They disturb neither me nor my neighbors.

WHY DO BEES SWARM?

A lot has been written about the swarming of bees and the swarm state in the literature and on the Internet. Often this is a retelling of the same considerations in one or another interpretation [19,20,21].

Books, the Internet, beekeepers, and scientists in one voice assert that swarming is an instinct of reproduction of bees.

Thus, having accepted this statement, we must agree that the reason for the transition of the bee family to the swarm state is a certain instinct of reproduction. Therefore, we (people) cannot manage this. It is not in our power. This is the call of nature. How can we control the instinct of reproduction? We are not Gods. Do you agree?

However, how are then the methods of stimulating artificial swarming consistent with the instinct of reproduction? For example, creation of a cramped hive and this causes bees to multiply. It is ridiculous! Something here does not add up. Don't you think so?

In my opinion, such an approach to this issue is fundamentally wrong. I deny this statement.

Bees family will never enter into a swarm state if the parameters of the bees' home and surrounding conditions meet their requirements. But in life, fortunately, it does not happen, and so the bees swarm, and this leads to their multiplication.

I take the liberty to assert, that the swarming of bees is a process caused by the instinct of survival.

When a bee family becomes unable to reside in specific conditions. For example, heat, crowding, humidity, cold, restless beekeeper. Bees cannot fully perform their tasks (read instincts). Then bees are forced to throw this place and fly away.

There are also such cases as abandoned completely empty beehives, but more often still the family turns into a swarm state and is divided into several families.

What happens to the bees that live in the wood in a hollow of a tree? Yes, nothing, until the volume of the cavity is completely filled with honeycombs and while the queen bee can lay eggs in them. No swarming for reproduction occurs.

When new wax combs have nowhere to be built. The wax cells from which the bees are born will be reduced, due to the remaining cocoons of previous births, to impropriety. That's when, to preserve the family and the species, the instinct of self-preservation starts working.

The bee family becomes a swarm and as a result, is divided into many families. New families populate new hollows in the trees. This is how the reproduction of bee colonies occurs in natural conditions.

Ideally, if we could provide a bee colony with an endless hollow, these bees would never have moved into a condition swarming. Fortunately, hollows have finite dimensions and therefore bees swarm and scatter to the world.

Well, you say, and what do we do about it? Is there an instinct of reproduction or self-preservation, what's the difference? The result is one and the same.

It is so, but if you accept the first thesis, then nothing can be done by a beekeeper, all because of nature, the call of ancestors, reproduction. All, sit and wait when the swarm comes out or apply all sorts of different methods to eliminate the swarming state.

For example, you agree with my statement: the swarming of bees is an instinct for self-preservation. Then, thinking about this slowly, you begin to understand what you need to do in order not to bring your colony of bees to the swarm state.

Have you already got a solution? I'm sure, yes. So I say that you just need to create comfortable conditions for the bees in the hives.

I took care of my bees and they have:

1. The house is spacious, not hot with proper sun protection, good ventilation, properly standing and

painted with the correct paint (I wrote about this earlier);

2. Respect to bees during honey extraction;

3. Fresh waxen honeycombs, a new wax;

4. Quiet surroundings around the hives;

5. Calm beekeeper, do not bother your bees with frequent inspection and permutations of frames with bee honeycombs.

I have created a comfortable environment for the bees. My bees do not swarm, since that time as my apiary began to be the freest apiary in the World. From the moment they became happy bees they have no time, they have a lot of work. Bees do not swarm and they can safely fulfill their important mission.

If I need to get a swarm or increase the number of bee's families, I do it simply. I call the swarm state "artificially". How to do it? Many know about this, one who does not know will find information in any reasonable book on beekeeping.

I want to draw your attention to the fact that by providing your bees with comfortable living conditions, without disturbing them in vain we can almost completely get rid of swarming. And most importantly, in my opinion, this is what we as beekeepers can manage consciously, and not be dependent on some kind of a case or some call of ancestors.

The adoption of such a view on the process of swarming allows the beekeeper to take a proactive position of conscious action based on an understanding of the causes of this phenomenon.

I can assume that the process of swarming, inherent dualism of the properties that cause it. On the one hand, it is the instinct of reproduction, since scientists are so eagerly talking about it. On the other hand, this is the instinct of self-preservation, of which I speak.

Perhaps in some conditions, the instinct of reproduction leads to swarming, in other conditions, swarming causes the instinct of self-preservation.

Now I write this way, only because this way scientists from beekeeping are constantly telling about it. Nevertheless, I emphasize that I do not agree with them. I still remain in my positions.

The swarming of the bees as a process is a consequence of the instinct of self-preservation of the bee family, and the reproduction of the bee family is a consequence of the process of swarming.

SUMMARY.

Swarming [19,20,21] is an instinct for self-preservation of a bee family. In other words, it sounds like that: the survival instinct of a bee family starts the process of swarming, and the result of the bees swarming is a reproduction.

This interpretation of the swarming of bees perfectly explains the methods proposed by science to stimulate artificial swarming. They are all based on the deterioration of the quality of life of bees in the hive. Have you paid attention?

Me and my bees like this explanation of swarming process. Without such an approach, I would not be able to make the bees happy. I provided my bees with comfortable living conditions in the hives. As a result, the swarming process bothers neither me nor my bees.

FOOD FOR HAPPY BEES

I will share my experience of preparing a tasty and useful feed for bees.

Sometimes there is a need to feed bees. To do this, there are many ready-made products and many recipes for cooking. I want to tell you how I do it. Perhaps, to some of you, my dear readers, my food recipe for bees will be interesting.

I assure you that bees will enjoy such tasty and useful food for sure. My bees like it. I know it. They quietly "told" me about it.

My technology of preparing food for bees

I prepare food at least 24 hours before the time of distribution. Sugar syrup is cooked on a broth of thyme (Thymus serpyllum) in it I add honey and citric acid.

Here is an example of preparing food for winter feeding. For instance, let it be, for a portion of five kilograms' sugar.

For this, I take 3,3 liters of water, 5 grams of citric acid, 2 tablespoons of honey and two generous bundles of dry herbs of Thymus serpyllum.

I weigh sugar. Then, I place it in an enameled container. Three liters of water in a separate container I warm to a boiling state. After the water is boiling, I throw in a container two generous bunch of grass and boil it for two, three minutes.

Then quickly through a fine sieve, I pour this decoction into a container with sugar. Same time, using a wooden spatula I constantly stir the solution until the sugar dissolves completely. Immediately I pour and dissolve the remaining water, in which I pre-dissolve 5 g of citric acid (1 g of citric acid per 1 kg of sugar).

Steadily I continue to stir this solution. When the temperature of the solution drops below forty degrees, I add two generous tablespoons of honey to it. Further, I continue stirring this solution until the honey dissolves completely. Then I cover the container with a lid and leave it for 24 hours.

Closer to the evening of the next day, I spend the distribution of food. Before distribution, food is heated to a temperature of 35-37 degrees, but no more. Further, as soon as possible (of course, if it is possible, it does not always turn out quickly) I send food to the hive.

Brief explanations of the technology for preparation of feed

Winter-feeding begins on August 10-15. The beginning of winter-feeding is justified by two reasons:

1. In the second half of August there is practically no food reserve in the surrounding nature in my region;

2. Increase the strength of the family. How I do it. I start to feed in the second decade of August and continue feeding until the end of the month. Thus, I stimulate the queen bee to actively lay eggs. This, in turn, leads to the build-up of the strength of the family by the bees in August. These bees will peacefully spend winter and grow young bees in the spring.

The ratio of water and sugar for winter top dressing is 1: 1.5, and for the spring 1: 1. The concentration of syrup for cooking is chosen not by chance. Scientists claim that it is with this concentration of syrup that the most sparing worker bees from wearing out involved in the processing of sugar syrup in honey occurs.

Adding natural honey to the syrup gives the food a pleasant honey aroma. At the same time,he enzymes that are in honey actively participate in the physicochemical processes taking place in this solution.

For example, in the literature, it is indicated that under the influence of the enzyme Invertase, sugar is converted into glucose and fructose. This enzyme is a part of honey. Undoubtedly, and other enzymes in honey, affect the properties of the resulting feed.

Within 24 hours the sugar syrup turns into something else. This is not just a syrup, it's a food with unique properties.

Adding citric acid to a sugar syrup leads to at least three positive effects:

1. The presence of acid in a sugar syrup prevents or partially reduces the crystallization of the obtained honey;

2. The presence of acid contributes to the process of decomposition of sugar on glucose and fructose;

3. Sour nutrition has a beneficial effect on the digestive tract of the bee. Promotes intestinal cleansing. This is especially important in the spring. Promotes an increase in the acidic reaction of the medium in the middle gut. This, in turn, leads to the fact that bees eating acidic feeding, on average, live longer.

The use of the aromatic herb Thymus serpyllum gives the food a peculiar taste and smell, which, apparently, the bees like. In addition, this herb has a colossal, health-enhancing effect which was tested by experience.

Once in spring, there fell sick and weakened a couple of families. Explicit signs of bee diarrhea. What to do? At that time I was a beginner beekeeper. No answer. I just listened to my intuition. I prepared a spring food for bees using the decoction of this wonderful herb.

The state of families has improved dramatically. Only two feeding and bees ceased to be sick, started to be active and soon caught up with the development of their neighbors. Since then, I have always been preparing all the food for bees only with the use of this herb.

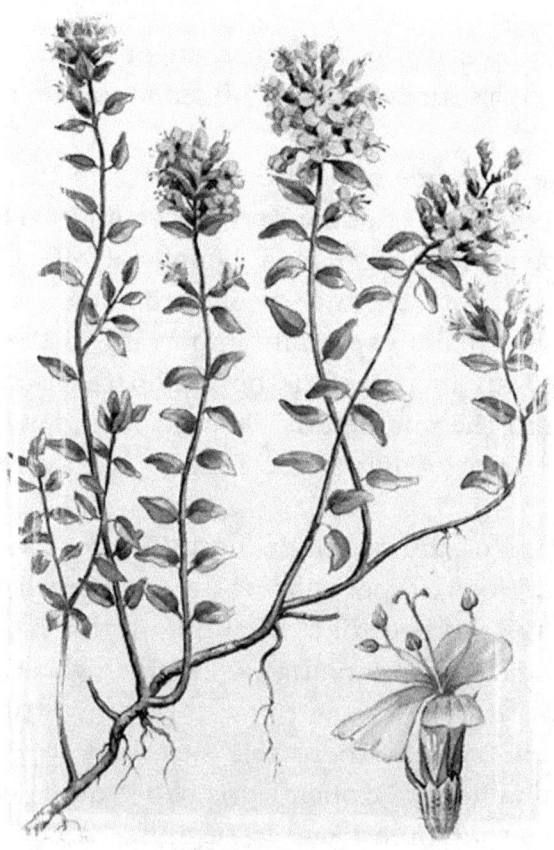

Thymus serpyllum.

And what a delicious tea with this wonderful and fragrant grass! Who tried it will agree with me. This is my favorite herb, probably because it smells like childhood. Every year in spring (the end of May) I go to harvest it.

This herb is plentiful in hilly places, on the southern slopes. I use it not only for bees and tea but also as a seasoning in my culinary experiments. Try it, and I'm sure you'll like it.

It's possible, this all my secrets for cooking delicious, fragrant and healthy food for my bees.

SUMMARY

I cook food for my bees out of sugar and honey with the addition of citric acid on the tasty and useful decoction of Thymus serpyllum herb. After 24 hours of exposure, this mixture turns into a fragrant, tasty and healthy product for my happy bees.

THE RAPID TRANSFER OF BEEHIVES

You probably know how experienced hunters or fishermen, gathering in a company, somewhere on the shore or in the field, like to talk about their trophies real or little fictional stories. In this case, all of these stories alive and are full at times of very funny details. Listening to such stories is a real pleasure.

Beekeepers keep up with the anglers and hunters. For example, on a nomadic apiary. After a hard day's work, they gather around the fire and tell different cases from their beekeeping practices.

Stories of beekeepers are not less funny and interesting than those of anglers or hunters. An attentive listener of such stories can learn many useful details from the practice of beekeeping.

So, in one of these companies, the old beekeeper told how he, in one evening transferred all his hives to a new place and did not lose any flying bees at all. Moreover, he argued that he placed the hives not far from the previous place. From his words, it turned out that the distance to the new "parking" of the hives was 50-100 meters.

The listeners laughed at him, and no one believed him. His story was called fantastic, and his arguments were unanimously rejected.

To me, his story did not seem fiction. Being an inquisitive person, at the first opportunity, I tried his method in practice. I confirm. The method works. I have tested it many times.

In the practice of a beekeeper, there are cases when it is necessary to rearrange the hives. This small task sometimes takes many days.

I remember when we did it with my dad, then "moving" the hive for 1 meter required 4-5 days. The process of beehive movement, as a rule, occurred in the evening. It was at a time when my friends and I were having fun on the street. I had to leave my friends and run to my father to help. Every time, when it happened, I was always upset.

According to my father's theory, moving a hive at a time should not be more than 10-20 centimeters. And it was done once at the end of the day when all flying bees gathered in the house. Probably, many now also move their hives.

Meanwhile, there is a simple and radical method for moving hives at a time, at any distance.

I move the hives together with my son. It is best to spend this event in the late evening, after the return of all flying bees.

We will immediately move the hive to a pre-prepared, new place. Then, on the landing board this hive I set an obstacle for the bees.

My bundle of wire.

The old beekeeper in his story mentioned dry grass and dry leaves. I am sure that in this case, the very element of the obstacle is important, the element of a novelty for bees.

Dry grass and leaves easily fly away from a small breeze. So I use a small bundle of wire. A bundle of wire can easily be fixed on a landing board. You can think of anything. For bees, an element of novelty is important.

The key to this method is that each time, encountering an obstacle at the exit from the hive, the bees check the settings of their "navigators" and adjust them anew.

In other words, bees behave like on the first flight. Watch and you will see for yourself. The movement of bees and the nature of the flight will be the same as during the first flight. This is confirmed by the fact that flying bees do not return to the old place, but are confidently sent to their hive in a new place.

In the old place, only those bees who would spend the night in the field will gather. As you know, there are few such so the losses will be insignificant.

However, if desired, you can also collect these bees in an empty, small hive. To do this, place an empty beehive with several waxen honeycombs, to the old place. And then we combine the collected bees with the bees in the beehive that was moved.

However, in my opinion, this is an unnecessary trouble. Bees return from the field home with honey and, after some time, they will be welcome in other hives.

That's how quick and easy I rearrange my hives. My bees did not complain about this method. Hence, the method is good.

SUMMARY

A significant obstacle for bees at the exit from the hive is the key to the method of rapid rearrangement. The presence of an obstacle causes the bees to reconfigure the coordinates of their "navigators". That is the whole trick. Works reliably.

MY NEW METHOD OF SPLITTING THE BEE FAMILY

In addition to the rapid re-installation of hives, the obstacle at the exit of the hive helps to quickly divide a bee family into two equal parts without losing flying bees (field bees). I always use this trick to divide a bee family into two equal parts.

You probably have already figured out how to do it.

Example: a bee family is well developed and as a result, there is no place in the hive. It is necessary to divide the family into two equal bee families.

How do I do this?

I prepare for this operation in the middle of the day, and the bee colony itself splits almost in the evening when the field bees (flying bees) return to their hive.

Preparation.

1. I'm examining the bee family and preparing it for splitting at the same time. I'm marking the wax frames that will go to the other hive. This can be done, for example, with colored chalk or construction tape. All bee family stocks (honey, pollen, bee brood) I try to divide exactly 1/2.

2. In order for the Queen bee remains in the original hive, I will insulate it with a mesh on a wax frame that will remain in the original hive.

Preparations are over.

<u>Splitting.</u>

In the evening, when almost all the flying bees have returned to their hive, I do the splitting operation. Quickly and without fuss, I reinstall all previously marked wax frames into a new empty beehive. Thus, we divide a large family into exactly one half.

The new beehive with half of the bees is located in a new place. Then, on the landing pad of the displaced hive, I set up an obstacle for the bees.

The process is completed. Bee family we split 1/2.

Tomorrow morning the field bees will meet the obstacle at the exit of the hive and reorient to a new location.

And let me draw your attention to the fact that we have separated the family without losing the flying bees. This is a very important point in the division of a bee family.

To get almost identical bee colonies, it is necessary to provide the newly created bee colony with a Queen bee.

I think about it in advance. I buy a new Queen bee or breed her on my apiary.

You can give the bees the opportunity to take care of their Queen, to grow it yourself. However, this is a topic for another story.

Now I'm describing the key to the method of quickly dividing bee colonies by 1/2 without losing field bees.

Here you have got a method of hives permutation! With a creative approach, it became clear that this is also the key to a new method of separating bee colonies without losing flying bees.

SUMMARY

The obstacle at the exit of the hive helps to split a bee colony into two equal parts, without losing the flying bees (field bees). I always use this trick to divide a bee family into two equal parts.

The main advantage of my method is the complete preservation of the field bees (flying bee) without the need to remove a new family of bees at a considerable distance from the parent hive.

SIMPLE AND CONVENIENT WATER DISTRIBUTION

In my bee farm, I use a simple and mainly convenient for bees drinking bowl.

The usual bottle is filled with water and covered with a thick soft cloth. Bees do not need to fly anywhere at all, "went out" quietly with "two buckets", scooped up and calmly returned to the hive.

It is convenient, the bees do not need to fly away.

It happens on hot days; the family can drain a bottle of water for a day. Perhaps filling bottles every day is hard, however, what won't you do for your favorite bees? It's not hard for me and it's even nice.

In addition, the rate of disappearance of water can assesses the state of affairs in the hive. If in a particular hive the water from the bottle began to decrease more slowly than before, then it is an occasion to look in the hive and to inspect the state of affairs of the family.

Observing, the rate of water decrease, in all drinking bowls on all the hives, it is possible to conduct a comparative analysis of the development of bee colonies on the apiary. Such an express analysis helps me to notice unforeseen changes in a particular hive.

Such drinking bottle is convenient for bees and is useful for an attentive beekeeper.

You can disagree with me, arguing that such drinking bottle is advisable to use in small home bee yards. However, this fact does not at all reduce the practical utility of this method of distributing water to bee colonies.

SUMMARY

Drinking bowl from a simple bottle simplifies the life of bees, and an attentive beekeeper can serve as an indicator of the state of affairs in the family of bees.

Drinking bowl for bees from a simple bottle causes pleasure to my bees. Therefore, I get only gratitude from them.

TREATMENT OF BEES FROM VARROA MITES

Varroa Mite is a small, reddish parasite that is of a size of a small pencil mark. The Varroa mite (VARROA DESTRUCTOR) is the most terrible pest for bee colonies all over the world. This destroyer is responsible for the death of millions of bee colonies every year.

For each beekeeper, it is extremely important to know, as the main thing, when to start treating bees from ticks. Certainly, It needs to be own methods of controlling the population from this parasite. For Determination of a bee family Invasion degree, there were developed experimental methods. Such as sugar shake method, sticky board method, alcohol wash method, drone brood inspection.

I will not here describe in detail the essence of all these methods, as they are perfectly illuminated in beekeeping literature and on the Internet. I only want to draw your attention to the fact that we cannot rely only on the visual inspection of our bees. We will not be able to see the vast majority of ticks, as they multiply and most of them are in the brood cells. One can't rely on visual inspection!

We need to apply a method or methods to quantify the degree of mite invasion. Even if these methods give a simple evaluation result of their application it is perfectly justified for the decision on the use of therapeutic and preventive measures.

I am mostly impressed by Sugar Shake Method, I use this method Because after its application all bees remain alive and this is the main thing for me and of course for my lucky bees.

I regularly check the presence of mites, many times during the season to determine when treatment is needed. How do I do that? I'm taking to shake of about 300 bees. It is about a ½ cup (measuring cup) of bees from the nesting framework on which the brood is. Then put these bees in a jar with a wide neck and close cover with mesh material sized 3X3 mm. Then through this "sieve" cover I add in the jar 2 or 3 tablespoons of sugar powder and shake it. I leave in peace for 5 minutes, then again shake it. Next, I turn the jar and shake the powder from the jar through the sieve cover on a blank white sheet of paper. Together with a powder the ticks Varroa fall out on a paper. Bees covered with powdered sugar return to the hive.

Then I count the number of ticks. If I find 9 or 10 Varroa, it is said that the level of infection is 3% i.e. 9 ticks/300 bees = 3 ticks per/100 bees. This is an alarm for me. I'm writing in a board magazine about the need for treatments. Generally speaking, I am concerned when the level of invasion is anything more than 2%.

Of course, you can not engage in control, but just regularly, for example, once a month to carry out medical events. But such an approach can lead to either unjustified financial costs or the loss of bee colonies because of the hidden global invasion which will develop gradually over several years. In most cases, the inability to control ticks Varroa in the hive will lead to a demographic explosion of ticks. And this will inevitably cause the death of a bee colony. I have seen in the literature information that the number of ticks Varroa in the colony will triple for a month when breeding only on the brood of working bees, and considering reproduction on the drone brood (drone brood) ticks' population can double every two weeks.

To date, there are several methods of treatment, but unfortunately, no one gives 100% result. Also, ticks quickly develop resistance for many common procedures, in other words, develop immunity to permanently applied means of chemical or biological treatment.

We all do not like to add chemicals to our hives, but the desire to avoid the processing of bees can lead to an explosion of mites at the end of the season and as a result complete death of the colony.

Therefore, I prefer an integrated approach to therapeutic and preventive measures. How is that? I try to use natural remedies together with drugs produced industrialists (Bio-pesticides).

In my practice for treatment I use mainly natural remedies such as grass Artemisia absinthium, grass Thymus serpyllum and crushed and dried root Horseradish.
Speaking, Essential Oil Thymus serpyllum is Thymol.

Artemisia absinthium.

Thymus serpýllum.

Horseradish.

Thymol is basicaly pesticides produced by the industry under the trademark Apilife WAS® containing a combination of essential oils thymol, eucalyptol, and menthol. This drug enjoys well-deserved popularity among beekeepers.

Grass Artemisia absinthium and grass Thymus serpyllum have a peculiar odor that Expels and even kills these parasites.

How do I apply these herbs to fight Varroa Mite? I apply smoke and spraying.

For the smoking of bees, in its Bee Smoker, I add a few chips of these herbs in dried form. In one case, I use a cocktail of these herbs and a shred dry root of a Horseradish. In another case, I use dry grass Artemisia absinthium, or dry grass Thymus serpyllum Together with dry crushed root Horseradish. This combination application of herbs, in my opinion, allows reducing the effect of Varroa Mite addiction to the components of these herbs.

In addition to using smoking for a bee colony, I apply to spray internal of the hive and at the same time spraying of bees by the steep broth of these herbs. The steep broth I prepare, if possible, from fresh grasses collected the day before in the nearest vicinities. Of course, if there is no fresh grass, then there goes dry grass. As in the case of bee smoker broth, I cook it from a cocktail of grasses or use each grass separately. And if to the bee smoker, I add grass Artemisia absinthium, then for spraying this time I prepare broth out Thymus serpyllum. At the next complex treatment, I use the opposite combination.

Separately I want to note that the dry root of horseradish I do not use for the preparation of broth.

In addition, I would like to draw your attention to the fact that I add these herbs and crushed the root of a Horseradish to bee smoker every time I have to use it. And this happens every time I inspect my bee colonies. Thus, always an examination of colonies, there is a prophylactic treatment of bees. As with treatment, I apply variable herbs in a bee smoker.

And so, we record the attention: I check worker bees as needed several times per season, and prophylactic every time when inspecting bee colonies. In addition to these natural remedies, after each treatment, I apply Bio-pesticides manufactured on natural components. This approach allows me to keep the Varroa Mite invasion level of a bee colony at a level of 1.5-2%.

SUMMARY

1. Varroa Mite at present Time represents the greatest threat to beekeepers and their colonies. Infected Colonies will perish unless measures are taken to control the level of the mite and the organization of medical and preventive measures.

2. A permanent monitoring of the Mite Invasion level allows the bee-grower to make informed decisions about when and what action is needed to combat Varroa destructor.

3. See the use of a single chemical product is likely to lead to the development of pest resistance. Several

different products should be used on a rotational basis.

4. You and only you can decide on when and how to treat bees from ticks. Your location and your opportunities play an important role in decision-making.

THE ERROR OF AN OLD BEEKEEPER

This story does not quite fit into the theme of this book about my happy bees, but it, in my opinion, is very instructive for young beekeepers. Although, as can be seen from the story, even experienced old beekeepers may not know about it.

I have met my old friend just recently. We have been acquainted with him for a long time since our youth. Although we live in one city, we see each other rarely, and our meetings are casual.

So it happened this time. We talked, exchanged news and accidentally came out on a common theme. It turned out that he and his father are engaged in beekeeping.

More precisely, he helps his father to work with bees. I was pleasantly surprised by this news and began to ask about the state of affairs on his apiary. The conversation brightened up because we talked about bees, and what could be more interesting...

So, Nicholas, this is my friend's name, told about a problem that he and his father could not solve.

The essence of the problem is next. In one of the hives a bee queen disappeared, family orphaned. Upon detection, they installed a honeycomb frame with bee honeycombs with freshly laid eggs. In order for bees, on their basis, were able to build the queen cell and grow out a new queen bee. It is clear. But what happened next?

After a while, having examined this frame with the honeycombs, they calmed down. On it, bees built and sealed several cells of the queen.

Everything was going according to the plan, but the next day the restless old beekeeper again conducted an inspection and was extremely frustrated because all queen cells were destroyed.

They repeated everything again. And this time all the events were repeated. The bees built queen cells, and then they were destroyed. What to do?

The beekeepers installed a frame with a ready, almost ripe, queen bee cell to speed up the process of breeding the queen bee. At the next inspection, the old beekeeper involuntarily became a witness of the exit of the young queen bee. Father and son rejoiced, and bees rejoiced along with them.

The life inside the hive warmed up, the activity of the flights renewed. Although the family weakened during this period, however, the appearance of the bee queen was felt both for bees and for beekeepers. What was the disappointment of the old beekeeper, when after a couple of days, the hive calmed down again, and there were signs of the bee family without a queen bee?

Moreover, after a vigilant inspection, my narrator found the dead queen at the bottom of the hive. Such was the story of my friend.

I asked Nicholas, whether he installed into a hive the honeycomb with fresh bee eggs and larvae either after the bees had built the queen cell or after the appearance of the young queen bee.

"Of course ..." - he replied in surprise. After all, it was necessary to restore the bee offspring, while in the hive there is no queen bee. With such an answer, I became aware of the reason for the unsuccessful attempts to deduce a new queen bee.

The matter is that at the beginning of my beekeeping, there was a similar problem. In those distant times, thinking about this situation, I found a solution to the problem. Look carefully.

What do we have in the starting position?

1. We do not have a queen. We need to grow a queen.

2.1. We install a sealed queen cell in the hive.

OR

2.2. we have a young queen bee, which still does not lay eggs.

3. To strengthen the family, we install bee honeycomb with bee brood and fresh eggs in a beehive.

Result: the bees immediately destroy the queen cells or kill the barren queen.

Why does it happen? Bees obviously "think", if we have fresh eggs, then we no longer need a queen bee.

The situation is not logical and unnatural. There cannot appear fresh bee eggs in a family where there is no queen bee. Do you agree? If they appeared, then there is already a queen bee and we do not need another. Is it logical?

Thus, by a desire to help the bee family, the beekeeper only complicates the life of the exhausted family.

This I told to my friend. He was very surprised by my story. Even a little indignant. Does not my father know about this? After all, he has got more than 60 years of beekeeping activity.

It turned out that he did not know. Obviously, before this time, he never got into such a situation. It seemed to me that the friend was not very happy about my story, although he promised to pass my advice to his father.

And the advice was simple. While the young queen bee has not begun to lay eggs, in no case in a beehive it is possible to establish frames with bee honeycombs on which there are fresh bee eggs.

Each time this will lead to the destruction of the barren queen bee. The same rule applies to bee queen cells. When a frame with honeycombs with fresh eggs and brood appears in the hive, the bees will destroy the queen cells.

Perhaps there are exceptions to this rule. Perhaps these exceptions have helped the old beekeeper not to fall into such a situation. I do not know about such exceptions. It was enough for me to step on these rakes once, not to repeat such experiments anymore.

But all the same, this case is directly related to my happy bees. Judge for yourself, If I do not get into this situation for many years, then my bees are all ok.

If I need to breed a young queen bee, then my bees do this without the above-described torments. Therefore, the life of my bees is very good.

Is it possible to say so? I think yes. Do you agree with this conclusion?

SUMMARY

If the young queen bee has not begun to lay eggs, in a beehive it is impossible to establish frames with bee honeycombs on which there are fresh bee eggs. Each time such an action will lead to the destruction of a barren queen bee or queen cell [**15,16,17,18**].

FINAL COLLECTIONS

My bees are the happiest bees ever. This I have repeatedly said throughout my short story. I hope that this story about my bees and me was for you cognitive, meaningful, interesting and, perhaps, sometimes cheerful.

I wanted to share with you my finds, tricks, methods, and views that helped me make my bees kind, friendly, efficient at work, calm and, undoubtedly, happy.

I am absolutely sure that all my methods are universal. Therefore, they can, to varying degrees, apply to hives of any design, on any apiary and in any conditions.

Throughout the narrative, I tried to draw your attention to some important points of practical beekeeping. All of them, without exceptions, in essence are fundamental to the well-being of bees.

Was I successful in this? It's up to you decide. Your right to use these findings or not, but the meaning and importance of my approach will not diminish from this fact. For me and my bees, so for sure.

All of them are tested in practice and brought me and my bees happy coexistence. With joy and with love in my heart, I give them to you.

With your permission, I will briefly list all that I have done for my bees:

1. I dyed the hives with a special "metallic" paint and achieved several important goals. Protected the

hive from adverse climatic influences. Allowed it to "breathe". Defended the bee colony from the influence of electric fields. I simplified the spatial orientation of the bees and provided the hive with a nice aesthetic appearance.

2. I set the hives in the best way. That allowed to increase the working time of bees. Eliminated adverse geopathogenic effects. Defended the bees from overheating on hot days and reduced the impact of atmospheric electricity on bees.

3. When extracting honey from hives, I do not create excessive anxiety for bee colonies. For this, I conduct preliminary preparation and use the principle of doctors - "do no harm". At the same time, I never extract all honey.

4. My simple drinker for bees from a simple bottle helps me to conduct a rapid analysis of the condition of colonies of bees. At the same time, bees easily and conveniently deliver water to the hive.

5. My method of rearranging hives makes life easier for me and for my bees. They calmly perceive this procedure.

6. In addition, it turned out that the key to the method of the rapid reinstallation can serve as a key to my new method of dividing the family of bees fifty on fifty without loss of flying bees. The main advantage of my method is the complete preservation of the field bee (flying bee) without the hassle of removing a new bee family to a considerable distance from the parent beehive. Here's to you along with the method of the hives rearranging! It turned out, with a creative

attitude, that it was also key to a new method of dividing a bee family.

7. My explanation of the process of bee swarming allows a beekeeper to take a proactive position of conscious action, on the basis of understanding the causes of this phenomenon. This explanation enables the beekeeper to consciously prevent the swarming state of bee colonies.

8. In my practice of fighting the Varroa mite (Varroa destructor) I prefer an integrated approach. To do this, I mainly use natural remedies such as Artemisia absinthium, Thymus serpyllum, as well as crushed and dried Horseradish root. In addition to these natural products, I use Bio-pesticides made from natural ingredients. This approach allows me to create an environmentally friendly space for my bees and at the same time successfully fight this parasite.

9. Finally, the food prepared on the basis of the decoction of the herb Thyme (Thýmus serpýllum) is delicious and healthy. In doing so, it works as a universal tool preventing bee diseases.

And I also wanted to draw your attention to my most important idea. I ask you, please read this carefully.

At all times, people kept bees for honey and bee products. That's OK. It has always been this way.

I suggest not to give up honey and everything that bees give us, but to change the very motive (reason) for the breeding of bees, especially in small bee yards.

And I would like to draw your attention to the fact that the idea of breeding bees to improve the natural environment makes sense and has a right to exist.

This approach does not require the refusal of honey, no way. It radically changes the relationship between a beekeeper and his bees. With this attitude, a bee becomes the center of attention, and honey - the result of its action.

This approach allowed me to make my bees happy. They calmly fulfill the tasks of harmonizing the surrounding nature. I am pleased to be aware of my involvement in bee magic, which fills the world with the love and harmony of life.

I propose not to look at bees as at a tool for extracting honey. Our bees are our good and faithful friends. Let us together with them, to the extent of their powers and abilities, make our World a better place. What do you say to that? I personally like this idea.

I will be glad if I managed it to draw your attention to the important points of which bee happiness is composed.

Let your bees be happy, and the world around you will be better.

Make your bees happy, and they will open to you the Joy of Life!

I wish you and your bees happiness, goodness, and health.

###

EPILOGUE

Here, the story of how I made my bees happy is over. I sincerely thank you for the fact that you have read my book to the end. I hope, that everyone has found for himself and for his bees, one or other useful information.

I will be grateful if you find time to share my thoughts about my work, about my approaches of a beekeeper. Your opinion is as important to me as for bees, the concern of a beekeeper.

Your thoughts and impressions can help other beekeepers to get acquainted with my book. I hope that this will increase the number of happy bees in our World.

I wish all of you, healthy and happy bees, fragrant honey and blue sky.

With respect and love to you
Peter Grayman

ABOUT THE AUTHOR

Peter Grayman is my pen name. Literally, I interpreted it as Peter the gray-haired man. Why is it so? Because I really am a gray-haired man.

I'm an engineer-physicist, from childhood I was drawn to technology, to devices and radio components. After serving in the army, I graduated from college in the field of technology microelectronic devices. Then the university is specializing in quantum radio-physics.

I used to work in various engineering groups and laboratories. I was fortunate enough to take part in the International Space Project "Phobos". The program featured cooperation of 14 nations, including Sweden, Switzerland, Austria, France, Germany, and the

United States. I worked in the group for the development and manufacture of some units and solar telescope units.

The telescope was mounted on the Phobos-1 satellite and perfectly fulfilled its mission of studying the sun.

I was not going to be a beekeeper at all. But life decided otherwise. Now I am a beekeeper amateur. I walked from beginner to the beekeeper who keeps his bees all right, in order to better life in the World.

My lucky bees safely fulfill their task of harmonizing nature. I am pleased to be aware of my involvement in the magic of bees, which fills the world with love and harmony of life.

LITERATURE

1. Natural electric field of the Earth
https://en.wikiversity.org/wiki/Natural_electric_field_of_t
he_Earth, Natural electric field of the Earth
https://encyclopedia2.thefreedictionary.com/Electric
+Field+of+the+Earth

2. Atmospheric electricity
https://en.wikipedia.org/wiki/Atmospheric_electricity

3. Aplin, K. L.; Harrison, R. G. (2013-09-03). Lord
Kelvin's atmospheric electricity History of Geo- and Space
Sciences. https://www.hist-geo-space-
sci.net/4/83/2013/hgss-4-83-2013.htmlmeasurements.

4. Fricke, Rudolf G. A.; Schlegel, Kristian (2017-01-
04). «Julius Elster and Hans Geitel – Dioscuri of physics
and pioneer investigators in atmospheric electricity».
History of Geo- and Space Sciences https://www.hist-geo-
space-sci.net/8/1/2017/.

5. Jean-Louis Le Mouël, Dominique Gibert, Jean-Paul
Poirier (2010). «On transient electric potential variations in
a standing tree and atmospheric electricity». Comptes
Rendus Geoscience 342: 95-9. Retrieved 2014-12-13.
http://citeseerx.ist.psu.edu/viewdoc/download;jsessionid
=5E2E5F96F124189FE599340E522C9B5C?doi=10.1.1.71
4.497&rep=rep1&type=pdf

6. R. S. Pickard «Bees, magnetism and electricity»
[1977] Pickard, R. S. Central Association of Bee-keepers
[Corporate Author]

7. Barbarovich Yu.K. Hives, bees and an electric field
/ A.N. Ivlev «In the wonderful world of bees», Lenizdat,
1988., http://www.paseka.org/v-chudesnom-mire-
pchyol/read#76

8. Bumble-bees use their fuzz to detect electric fields
http://physicsworld.com/cws/article/news/2016/jun/07/bumblebees-use-their-fuzz-to-detect-electric-fields

9. Bees and electric field
http://www.emfs.info/effects/agriculture/bees/

10. Ernst Hartm ann: Journal weather-ground-human, issue 5-2002, How it all began - The importance of the pathogenic irritation lines in the medical practice.

11. The magnetic field of the earth Lattice structures of the earth magnetic field,
http://erdmagnetfeld.pimath.de/global_grids.html
Copyright © Klaus Piontzik

12. Earth Rays , https://swissharmony.com/earth-rays/

13. GEOPATHIC STRESS by Richard Creightmore,
https://www.landandspirit.net/html/geopathic_stress.html

14. Geopathic Stress and the Optimal Location of Beehives according to the Principles of Geomancy,
https://www.landandspirit.net/html/beehive-location.html

15. Bees get a buzz out of electricity from flowers
https://www.mnn.com/earth-matters/animals/stories/bees-get-a-buzz-out-of-electricity-from-flowers

16. Bees Can Sense the Electric Fields of Flowers
http://phenomena.nationalgeographic.com/2013/02/21/bees-can-sense-the-electric-fields-of-flowers/

17. Walsh, Bryan (7 May 2013). «Beepocalypse Redux: Honeybees Are Still Dying — and We Still Don't Know Why». Time Science and Space. Time Inc. Retrieved 21 June 2013.
http://science.time.com/2013/05/07/beepocalypse-redux-honey-bees-are-still-dying-and-we-still-dont-know-why/

18. Beekeeping collection at the National Library of Scotland https://digital.nls.uk/moir/

19. Villa, José D. (2004). «Swarming Behavior of Honey Bees (Hymenoptera: Apidae) in Southeastern Louisiana». Annals of the Entomological Society of America. 97 (1): 111–116. doi:10.1603/0013-8746(2004)097[0111:SBOHBH]2.0.CO;2 https://academic.oup.com/aesa/article/97/1/111/11469

20. Avitabile, A.; Morse, R. A.; Boch, R. (November 1975). «Swarming honey bees guided by pheromones». Annals of the Entomological Society of America. 68 (6): 1079–1082. DOI:10.1093/aesa/68.6.1079 https://academic.oup.com/aesa/article/68/6/1079/47316

21. Seeley, Thomas D.; Visscher, P. Kirk (September 2003). «Choosing a home: How the scouts in a honey bee swarm perceive the completion of their group decision making». http://bees.ucr.edu/reprints/bes54.pdf

22. Biolocation, Dowsing https://wikivisually.com/wiki/Dowsing, https://en.wikipedia.org/wiki/Dowsing

www.ingramcontent.com/pod-product-compliance
Lightning Source LLC
Chambersburg PA
CBHW070434290526
45791CB00005B/1966